SPLIT

MOMENT

SPLIT

MOMENT

Thomasema Pannell

Author

Copyright © 2022 by Thomasema Pannell.

All rights reserved. This book or any portion thereof may not be reproduced or used in any manner whatsoever without the express written permission of the publisher and author except for the use of brief quotations in a book review.

Printed in the United States of America

First Printing, 2022

ISBN: 978-1-951883-51-5

The Butterfly Typeface Publishing
PO Box 56193
Little Rock AR 72215

www.thebutterflytypeface.com

Dedication

This book, "Split Moment" is dedicated to my children and the children who I mentor and raised by the grace of God. They all call me, "Mom."

I thank you for being my children. As your parent, you drive me crazy, and I love you at the same time. You will never be too old to listen to my voice; I'm going to talk anyway. I will listen, and ultimately, I get the last word. I pray the last word is the word that supports your needs.

When I think of family- I think of you:

My children: Rod, Kaila, Isaiah, Isaac, Chase, Porshia, Jennifer, and Nakia

Rod, Kaila, Isaiah, and Isaac, walk in truth and remember – You can't call everyone friend. Everyone in your face is not your friend.

My nieces: Charrelle, Arrielle, Destany, and Ta'Kerra

My nephew: Chris

My great nephews: Jayden, Christian, and Kannon

My great niece: Janiyah

My Goddaughter: Victoria

Tribute – IN MEMORY OF MY FRIEND

Dr. (Sheriff) Heubert Peterkin

A friend that will be missed is an understatement. Journey with me…. Phenomenology research focuses on first-hand "lived experiences," All who experienced a common personal phenomenon. As we process the internal dialog about the "lived experiences" phenomenon. The common internal feeling we All have experienced in one word "LOVE". Love that he gave to All. A man that I can call friend and not have a title attached. This great man was born a son. He was raised as brother. He matured into husband. He learned how to father. He was God- Father. He was Grandfather. He was Sherriff. He was Doctor. You see… This great man was birthed into a title and earned other titles along the way. This great man was humble and careful with his titles; titles that didn't make him a person. The person inside of him; made the title. This great man gave many a common "lived experience"; one word "LOVE." This great man that I personally called "PeePete" was my friend, loved my children (Rod, Kaila, Isaiah and Isaac) and the community at large. He was a Soldier.

By Thomasema Pannell

Author, USA (Ret.)

Contents

Daily Inspiration to Self-Awareness	1
Leadership	3
Leaders Are What We Are	4
Story Time: Leadership	5
Purpose of the story	6
For discussion	6
Poem	10
Story Time: Reality	11
Purpose of the story	13
For discussion	14
Story Time: Trust	16
Purpose of the story	17
For Discussion	17
Story Time: Choices	18
Purpose of the story	19
For Discussion	19
Split Moment Exercise 1: Icebreaker	21
Quote	27
For discussion	28
Removing Self-Imposed Barriers/ Missing words	30
Removing Self Imposed Barriers - Exercise 2: Goals	31
Removing Self Imposed Barriers - Exercise 2a: Open Dialogue	32
Removing Self Imposed Barriers - Exercise 2b: The 4 Ps	33
Split Moment Exercise 1: Ice Breaker (Answer Key)	35
Journal	37
Thomasema Pannell, Biography	57

Foreword

Split Moment was created from experiences of real-life situations. This book is for adults and teens. Most often we say, "It can't happen to me," or we have an attitude that we are untouchable. The truth is life happens in a split moment.

The stories are true experiences that both adults and teens can relate to because they would've either experienced some of the traumatic experiences, or they know someone who has been through the traumatic experience.

This book is geared to support parents in communicating with their child(ren) and for adults to open communication with their spouses and bring awareness to their children, families, and friends in potentially enduring as life happens with growth.

The book is for people 16-years-old and up. This age group is selected because it's a crucial time in a young man or woman's life where they begin to think they have it all figured out! For the young man and young woman, this information is being brought to the forefront because I believe, many times, our children experience life before they're ready all because parents are in denial, not accepting them, ignoring them, not taking the time to listen to them, and refusing to hear their children's voices. Well, let me tell you, young people, most parents are doing the right thing. Parents are mentoring, communicating, sharing their own lived experiences, and YOU are not listening. YOU'RE not hearing because these factors covered in this book are for awareness and for being intentional about adding values to others and sharing from the heart.

I need to mention, the scenarios in the storyline are not reflective of my children or a direct reflection of any family member. My four children and family members are in the same age group. This book was created in thought three years ago. However, I will discuss how I could've lost my daughter to a car accident in a "Split Moment." The situation was a direct reflection of how we are faced with the unknown, and many experiences in the unknown can be life changing. As a parent, I'm faced with these very topics and trying to ensure that my children can hear my voice and minimizing the mistakes that can potentially occur in a "Split Moment."

My writing ability allows for God to speak to me and pour out wisdom that comes to my spirit. As you think about how and why things happen in a "Split Moment," stop and think. Peer pressure limits your ability to see when you ignore the truth. Just for a few minutes, think about your current walk and where you are in the right now moment. Watch the words that flow from your mouth. You must be an example of what love should be like; leave the negative attitude behind. Let it go and walk into your destiny. Time is of the essence, and time waits for no one. Each day, each hour, each minute is your journey. Take the time to pray, be persistent, be patient, and have perseverance over your life. Speak life into existence and walk by faith.

Acknowledgments

Late Pastor, John D. Fuller, Sr., always said, "When you start calling out folk names and you miss one... they will let you know it......." Many words of wisdom, to stay safe. Not all names can be mentioned in this book; you are not forgotten.

Dr. (Senior Pastor) Christopher Stakehouse, First Lady Savannah, and Family, thank you for being the example for our church Lewis Chapel Missionary Baptist Church (LCMBC), Fayetteville, NC. Thank you for your prayers, insights, and extended love over the years, thank you.

Pastor, C. David Stackhouse and Lady Ranee, peace and love, I have one word that represents how I feel for you both "love," the love that you display for each other, the community, and the church at large.

LCMBC-West, I love each of you and pray blessings over your lives.

LCMBC At large - Prayer Warriors, Music Ministry, all governing sites, and members, over the years, friendships have been built and treasured memories have been made. [There are too many of YOU to name one by one. If you are a member. I'm talking about you. Thank you for being a loving, inspiring, and wonderful church family.] During the bereavement of my mother and family members – YOU were right there with me and my children. I love each of you.

Rev. Garland Pierce, Representative, District 48, North Carolina House of Representatives, thank you for your encouragement and mentorship. Continue to serve the community while adding value to others. I have watched you labor; rewards are given to those who work without selfish service. Many blessings to you and your family peace and love friend.

Tammy B. and son, Marcellus, I thank God for having both of you in my life and my children's lives. Tammy is a dedicated sister and friend. You are loving, straightforward, and trusted. We have laughed, cried, and shared life stories as they happen. We have a book to write. My friend, when you took the oath to defend and serve, indeed you have honored that oath and continued to serve. I'm waiting on retirement, so we can travel and see the vision come true. I love you, my sister and friend.

Marcellus, I watched you grow from elementary school to college level. I'm proud of your accomplishments. Continue to walk in truth; continue to gain all the higher education you can obtain. Remember everyone, that smile in your face is not your friend. Friends are few and far between. Trust your mother and continue to love her with all your heart. I love you. Auntie...

More Acknowledgments

Ketha, thank you for being a listener over the past 31 years. I know your ears are burning, and I probably gave you hearing loss! Trust your inner love for "Bell Keepsake," and let it blossom. As you say, "Assortment" in short. One day people will know what that means. We have a book to write. I love you, friend.

Porshia, H., what can I say about you and your son, Avery? Your art skills get me every time. No matter where the military sent us, we kept in touch. Years have gone by, and you're still here. My friend of over 15 years, you're stuck with me. Get used to it. Pack your bags. We have some highway to burn up. We have a lot in common. We have a book to write. I love you, friend.

Wanda, L., my dear Sister in Christ, I love you and your family. I love the family dynamics and peace you all bring to my family. Thank you for sharing Momma with me. Love you, friend.

Darryl P., what an amazing man you are to the community. Thank you for being that [Father Guide] to my family. You're my brother and friend indeed. Much love, friend.

Spencer LaC., when I think of smooth riches, you come to mind. Thank you for your wisdom and mentorship. You're a value in the community and are always thinking of others. All things will blossom in the near future. Peace and love, my friend.

What a big heart you have for the love of brother and sisterhood. Thank you for supporting me and always being there to mentor and listen. Much appreciated from my heart to yours, love you, brother and friend.

New York Family: I always tell people never to forget where your beginning started. Always acknowledge your foundation, Roosevelt, Long Island, New York.

To all of my family and friends from Roosevelt, Jr. – Sr. High School and the surrounding area, there are too many of you to name one by one. Class of 1985 – Rough Riders, Exit 21... Much love and I'm proud of all that you accomplished in your goals and journey in life. Place your name here in the blank space_____. I love you all, classmates and friends.

Sojourner Truth, Tent #770: Fayetteville, NC, President and Sisters, I love each of you. My God continues to pour out blessings and to watch over the works of our ancestors. Continue serving and adding value to others.

North Carolina, Prince Hall Affiliate, Order of the Eastern Star: I love you all. Continue the works of serving and adding value to others.

Authors: Thank you for sharing words of encouragement as I shared my journey to write. Thank you for allowing me to mentor some of you to your journeys, and I thank you for supporting the community with your grace and words of inspiration.

To know each of you on a personal level, I'm blessed.

Spencer L. Duffey, "Others Lord, Life, and Legacy of Lorine C. McLeod"

Dennis Biddle, "Secrets of the Negro Baseball League"

Betty Kilby Fisher, "Wit, Will, & Walls"

Georgia Hooker McNeill, "God Gave Me Kinky Hair"

Late Dr. Sherriff A. Hubert A. Peterkin, "How to Stop For a Cop"

Dr. Walter R. McCollum, PhD, "Strength of a Black Man: Destined For Self-Empowerment"

Dr. Patrice J. Carter, "Superb Woman, From Bad Girl to God's Girl"

Paul J. Williams, "I Witness – A Family Tragedy"

Tre'vone L. McNeill, "Wake Up!"

John C. Maxwell, "Invaluable Laws of Growth"

Kimothy Monroe, "Monster Eyes"

Dr. Diran L. Cowell, "Through The Walls – Without Any Doubting or Quiddit"

Kimberly Deneen, "It's Only A Flower – I'd Rather Play Video Games"

Dr. Alvin Parker, "Stronger Than Pride"

Rev. Lettie Ar- Rahmaan, "Struggling To Be Me – No Longer Silent & Invisible At The Table"

Military: To my military friends, thank you for leading from the front. I love each of you. There are too many to name one by one; however, you're not forgotten.

General Mitchell Kilgo, thank you for being in my life for over 35 years. Our beginnings at Virginia Union University will always be treasured and remembered. Your love, friendship, mentorship, and journey have been a blessing. Thank you for your continued service and dedication to the military community. Peace and love always. I love you, friend.

Daniel, B., thank you for being in my life for over 28 years. You're a tough and faithful friend. No matter how many of your birthdays I miss, you're still here. Thanks for loving me and the family over the years. Your calls, letters, flowers, and visits are truly treasured. You blessed me with your presence when my mother passed, and I can truly call you FRIEND. Much love, friend.

Larry, J., I call you friend. I'm still the BOSS. You haven't figured that out yet! It's been 20 years. I need a prize for just being your friend. (Laughing) I love you, friend.

Daily Inspiration to Self-Awareness

"Removing Self-Imposed Barriers."

"Reach One – Teach One."

"I Can. I Will. I Must."

"Who Am I? Who Are You? Who Are We?"

"I Am Me. I Am Me. I Am My Own Black Me."

"I Can. I Will. I Must."

John Maxwell capitalized on these three words that empowered people "encouragement, connect, and love."

I encourage you to take one step at a time. "Lean in – Lean into the message. Engage in your community, amplify your impact, and do it now." I ask a question in my workbook journal, "Denton Place – Tables Turned, Letters From The Heart." Question: "How Well Do You Know Yourself." Just take a minute and think about what I'm saying. "How Well Do You Know Yourself" – Journey with me.

Understand that success has a price – it's not convenient. You will be lonely; you will feel alone. However, the decisions that we make will show up in our lives. I encourage you to seek to find your purpose. What do I mean by find your purpose? We all have a gift. You already have the answer; don't be afraid. Step out towards your destiny and journey to your success.

Once you're encouraged, then you must connect. Connect to your passion. Whatever your passion is, identify with it. Channel your thoughts and behavior to link your connection to what I consider to be your dream. We have dreams. Is that right? How many of us have dreams? Encourage, connect, and now love. Love - What is love? Love has various definitions. Love can be seen, heard, and felt. In the workbook journal, "Denton Place – Tables Turned, Letters From The Heart"- Love, love is kind and patient. It's pure. It's meaningful, and most of all - You are all loved. That's my purpose today, to let you know that you are loved. Be a leader; show your leadership. Encourage someone to connect with his purpose and love each other.

We all have a story. We all have challenges, and we all have roads that lead to success. We are all leaders. Leadership - we are all leaders in our daily activities. Step out in faith and know that if you take one step – many more steps will follow.

Leadership

President Joe Biden and Vice President Kamala Harris:

The people listened, and God has spoken.

Thank you for your leadership of all people.

Leaders Are What We Are

Let your word be your word and your actions be your works!

LEAD

LEAN (lean in & support your community)

EMULATE (be that example by your character & walk)

AMBITIOUS (being intentional about your actions)

DETERMINED (never give up or quit no matter how difficult things become; stay determined, motivated, strong, & keep your faith in all you do)

LEADER

LOVE (patient, caring & sharing, devotion, giving, & understanding)

EASY (peace of mind)

ATTITUDE (shows character, shows positive in a negative setting which goes back to patience) We all know how that can be. If you agree, say AMEN.

DISCIPLINE (redirect the way we do things; be STERN)

EAGER (being ambitious & not losing focus)

RESPECT (demand it with positive interactions & respect to the Word of God.)

Story Time: Leadership

While walking in the VA Medical Facility parking lot, I encountered a fellow veteran named Sutton.

He spoke and we began a conversation. We came to understand that we shared a passion for people. I told him about my books and that I was among other things, a published author. I gave him my card.

He said, "I never met a real black author. I don't have money today, but I ask that you trust me."

A few weeks later, I called him to check on his health. He would call me from time to time as well just to chat.

A couple of things to note:

- I never mentioned money to him. (leadership quality)
- I never ignored his calls. (leadership quality)

One day I opened my PO Box to find a package from veteran Sutton that included a beautiful piece of art inscribed with the following words:

He's the joy of my salvation.

And on the back side were the words:

Thomasema Pannell, author

Purpose of the story

Sometimes there is value in people that we may not see right away. Not all value is monetary. Doing the right thing just because it is the right thing to do is a habit we should form. You may be rewarded as I was in this story or you may not. However, the real reward is in treating others the way you would want to be treated.

For discussion

1. How many times have you stopped to talk to a stranger?
2. Do you perform random acts of kindness?
3. Do you think the package I received was worth more than the cost of a book?
4. Explain your answer to number 3.
5. What is the lesson in this story for you?

Poem

I Am Me - My Own Black Me

Who am I? Who are you?

Nobody cares, but somebody does.

My hair is kinky, not straight; my nose wide, narrow, or round.

Who am I? Who are You?

My legs bow, my backbone low, I'm walking fast yet slow.

Rise up! Stand up! Let no one shut you up.

Speak loud and always look up to the cloud. Skies tell a story; I give GOD glory.

Little boy, little girl you're precious as a giant pear.

My eyes cry won't stay dry.

My heart is pure; my faith is secure.

I must fight in this world of hate; my GOD is never late.

The cause is just, my love's a must.

My skin is different; my dreams are big.

My vision is clear; you go, my dear.

My brothers and sisters of the world, stand together.

Support each other.

Who am I? Who are you?

I Am Me - My Own Black Me.

-Author, Thomasema Pannell

Story Time: Reality

Coronavirus Disease 2020: It Can't Happen to Me

January 1, 2021, I looked forward to starting a new year with high expectations and positive outlooks. I looked forward to having our lives back as the vaccine was becoming a true reality. I thought things would begin to reverse back to the normal standard of living prior to the onset of Coronavirus Disease (COVID-19).

My hopes were shattered when I received a phone call from my 21-year-old daughter.

"Mom, I'm not feeling well.

Kaila and I spoke daily so her call wasn't unusual. However, what she had to tell me was anything but usual.

"It's been four days now and I have fever off and on. My throat hurts and my eyes are sensitive to light. My body aches and I'm not eating much," Kaila explained. "But I don't think it's anything serious. I took a shower on Tuesday night and then ran out to the store in a light jacket. Once I got to the store, I realized how cold it was and maybe that wasn't a good idea to be out so soon after a shower."

"What? Are you crazy? How many times have I told you to wear more clothes," I said in my mom voice. "It's no wonder you are sick. Figure it out."

But then I had a horrifying thought.

"Wait, where have you been in the last five days?" I asked. "Have you gotten tested for COVID-19 like I've been asking you to do?"

Silence.

"Kaila, this thing is real."

Still no response.

"The germ has no name on it," I continued. "Where in the world have you been over the past several days?" I repeated. I was frustrated now. Why is it that young adults and teens have a problem sharing information with their parents?

The line is still silent.

"Kaila, I need you to start backtracking your activity," I insisted. "What have you been doing? You said there was someone you knew who had a family member who had tested positive. Were you around them? Did they get tested? What were the results," I continued to ask questions.

Finally, Kaila replied, "No, still waiting on a call."

"Well, I hope you are not depending on someone else's results to dictate your health," I pushed. "Well, let me tell you something. This thing is real. The virus has no name on it and has no respect for age. You have some of the symptoms of COVID-19. I'm telling you now. Schedule an appointment at Fort Bragg today. Go somewhere. Get the test. I mean it. You can't come home until you get tested. It's no joke." I was serious and Kaila knew it.

"Ok. Ok. I will." Kaila replied.

"Don't ok me," I said fully upset now. "I'm hanging up now. Call and schedule two appointments. Get a rapid test AND follow up with your primary doctor. I mean it. Call me back after you make the appointment," I insisted.

The next day, the appointment was scheduled. Kaila went to the appointment. I got a phone call around 5:00 pm.

"Hey, Mom, I got the results back."

"Really," I asked. "What were the results?"

"You really want to know?" Kaila questioned.

"Really," I respond, "You are asking me that?" I replied.

"The results are POSITIVE." Kaila stated.

"What! Are you telling me the truth?" I couldn't believe it. "I need to see the results. Where is the paper? Did you get the results in writing? I need to see. Really, are you playing? Kaila, stop, tell the truth." I was frantic.

"For real." Kaila said in a small voice.

Purpose of the story

Kalia didn't think it could happen to her. She attended a closed-in social gathering with an unknown number of attendees in an unknown location. The outcome was POSITIVE to COVID-19. This reckless behavior is unacceptable. The family could've been exposed, and innocent people could have been infected by all those in attendance. The virus is real, and it affects everyone differently.

Please stay home, follow the guidelines set forth by the medical experts, and stay alive.

For discussion

How could this situation have been avoided?

Do you believe the daughter was aware of the reckless behavior?

Do you believe the age group between (18 – 25) is misguided?

Do you believe the daughter learned a lesson in the situation?

Do you think it's imperative that young adults should listen to their parents?

What advice would you recommend to parents and caregivers of young adults?

What advice would you give the daughter?

What actions can be taken to ensure young adults understand the virus is real?

Story Time: Trust

Money on the Desk

Scarlet was a young lady working at a bank. She worked in custodial duties. She had been working at the bank in the evenings for six years. As Scarlet mopped the floor, she noticed a dollar bill on the desk. She was a young lady with low income. She had little to no money in her purse. Her car fuel was low, and here she was looking at the money on the desk.

Scarlet thought for a moment, *Maybe I can take the money, put it in my pocket, and continue working.*

In that "Split Moment," she had to make a decision. That decision tested her work position. It could've given her the money she needed, or she could've continued working and just accepted that her money was low.

Scarlet, in this moment, decided to keep working and to leave the money on the desk. It was surely tempting for her to take the money, get gas, and pretend that nothing happened. However, her decision not to touch the money was the best thing she could do. She was free of guilt. She was faithful to her decision not to touch the money, and it showed that she was loyal to her company policy.

The next day, Scarlet's supervisor called her into the office.

"You passed the test," her supervisor said.

"What test," Scarlet asked, confused.

"You were put to the test," her supervisor responded. "I wanted to see if I could trust you for a promotion."

Purpose of the story

Scarlet's supervisor wanted to see if Scarlet could be trusted with more responsibility. She wanted to promote Scarlet to a position that would expose Scarlet to even more money. Scarlet proved that she was loyal and could be trusted. What you do when you think no one is watching matters!

For Discussion

1. How do you think Scarlet handled herself?
2. Do you think Scarlet was going to take the money?
3. Do you think her decision to leave the money was good?
4. What would you have done?
5. Do you think the supervisor was fair to test Scarlet?
6. Do you think Scarlet would accept the promotion?
7. Do you think Scarlet deserve to be put in that situation?
8. How do you feel about the money on the desk?

Story Time: Choices

Walking from The Corner Store

Jerry got up on a normal day. He decided to walk to dry cleaners to pick up his dress shirt and to stop by the corner store. Jerry decided to get a bag of chips and soda. The corner store was located approximately 15 minutes away from his home. It was a dry and warm day. As Jerry walked down the sidewalk, he noticed that an unmarked police car had rolled slowly behind him for 1 or 2 blocks. Jerry realized by the time he had stepped of the sidewalk to cross the street. The unmarked police car turned really quickly in front of him to block him from walking. Next, he noticed that there were 5 to 6 marked police cars blocking him. There were at least 10 to 15 undercover and uniformed police officers who surrounded the young man.

Jerry began to yell, "Hey, what are you doing? I haven't done anything?"

The police yelled to the young man, "Hold your hands up."

Jerry was confused and replied, "Hey, what are you doing? I've been home all day."

The police yelled, "What's your name? Where are you coming from?"

Before the young man could answer, the police were in his face yelling, "You look like someone who committed a robbery."

The yelling continued from both sides, and finally, people were out of their homes looking and trying to figure out what was going on. Jerry's father was home, and he came out with disbelief as to what was happening.

Jerry kept his hands in the air. Although the situation was frightening, he and his dad had talked about how he should conduct himself in such a situation. Jerry knew not to make any sudden moves and to obey the officer's request.

Jerry's father heard the commotion and came outside. He quickly identified Jerry and verified that he was home all day, and that Jerry just went to pick up his dry cleaning.

Jerry felt betrayed because of the color of his skin. He knew the police only stopped him because he was African American. Jerry thought to himself, why do black men have such a hard time? Why are we always a target? Why do the police always say, "You look like someone that just robbed..."?

Purpose of the story

What we do when we feel mistreated or wronged matters. It is important to talk about the things that happen and make a plan so that if/when you are faced with tough choices, you will react based on knowledge rather than fear.

For Discussion

1. How do you think Jerry handled the police?
2. Do you think the police were wrong for following the young man for 1 or 2 blocks?
3. Do you think racism played a role in the sidewalk block?
4. Why do you think police harass young black males?
5. What do you think could've happened if Jerry's father was not home?
6. How do you feel about the stop?
7. What is your emotion?
8. Could Jerry have done anything differently?

Split Moment Exercise 1: Icebreaker

Directions: On the next few pages, look for words within the words "SPLIT MOMENT."

Log your times for 30, 60, and 90 seconds and list your times here:

(Use a timer, a stopwatch, or a clock to monitor your time.)

30 seconds: _____

60 seconds: _____

90 seconds: _____

Best Time: _____

(30 seconds)

S	P	L	I	T
STOP	PRESSURE	LIMIT	IGNORE	TRUTH

M	O	M	E	N	T
MINUTE	OBSERVE	MOUTH	EXAMPLE	NEGATIVE	TIME

Use this space to write your words.

1.
2.
3.
4.
5.
6.
7.
8.
9.
10.
11.
12.
13.
14.
15.
16.
17.
18.
19.
20.
21.
22.
23.
24.
25.
26.
27.
28.
29.
30.

(60 seconds)

S	P	L	I	T
STOP	PRESSURE	LIMIT	IGNORE	TRUTH

M	O	M	E	N	T
MINUTE	OBSERVE	MOUTH	EXAMPLE	NEGATIVE	TIME

Use this space to write your words.

1.
2.
3.
4.
5.
6.
7.
8.
9.
10.
11.
12.
13.
14.
15.
16.
17.
18.
19.
20.
21.
22.
23.
24.
25.
26.
27.
28.
29.
30.

(90 seconds)

S	P	L	I	T
STOP	PRESSURE	LIMIT	IGNORE	TRUTH

M	O	M	E	N	T
MINUTE	OBSERVE	MOUTH	EXAMPLE	NEGATIVE	TIME

Use this space to write your words.

1.
2.
3.
4.
5.
6.
7.
8.
9.
10.
11.
12.
13.
14.
15.
16.
17.
18.
19.
20.
21.
22.
23.
24.
25.
26.
27.
28.
29.
30.

Quote

"You may see me struggle, but with god you will never see me fall."

-Kaila Parsons

For discussion

What are your thoughts and feelings about the quote? Write down (4) things that you consider to be a struggle.

1._____

2._____

3._____

4._____

How do you think you can face the struggles? Write down (4) things that you have accomplished.

1._____

2._____

3._____

4._____

How is your faith when you're challenged with actions of despair? Write down (4) things that guide your faith.

1._____

2._____

3._____

4._____

Removing Self-Imposed Barriers

The following exercises are designed to help you develop self-awareness and to remove any barriers that impede your emotions. Remove anything or any people in your life that cause you pain and uncertainty. Let go of anyone who does not listen to your voice and fails to communicate. Think of yourself and bring awareness to your innermost feelings. Recognize the things that you impose on yourself and analyze the steps necessary to overcome.

In my book, "Denton Place – Tables Turned, Letters From The Heart," there is a section titled, "Get To Know Yourself." I added this section because as I reflected over my life, I found myself asking, "Would things have been different in my personal life if I had better communication skills?"

Take time to get know yourself. Ask yourself and those around you questions in an effort to gain greater awareness and understanding.

Questions to consider:

1. How well do you know yourself?

2. Can you look in the mirror and be honest with yourself?

3. How do you remove self-imposed barriers?

Removing Self-Imposed Barriers
Exercise 2: Goals

Write (18) things that you would remove from your daily activities and life.

1. _____
2. _____
3. _____
4. _____
5. _____
6. _____
7. _____
8. _____
9. _____
10. _____
11. _____
12. _____
13. _____
14. _____
15. _____
16. _____
17. _____
18. _____

Removing Self-Imposed Barriers
Exercise 2a: Open Dialogue

Dialogue within groups or individuals to discuss the areas of "Removing Self Imposed Barriers." Open dialogue (15 minutes)

Removing Self-Imposed Barriers
Exercise 2b: The 4 Ps

Prayer, persistence, patience, and perseverance can assist you in removing self-imposed barriers. Discuss the questions below.

Prayer

1. How do you pray?
2. Why do you pray?
3. Why is prayer important?

Persistence

1. Should you ever give up?
2. Why do you think it's positive or negative to be persistent?
3. What does Persistence mean to you?

Patience

1. Why should we have patience?
2. Why is it important to be patient?
3. How would you define patience?

Perseverance

1. What does perseverance mean to you?
2. Have you ever had been delayed in achieving success?
3. Give an example of something delayed or difficult that you overcame with success.

Split Moment Exercise 1: Ice Breaker (Answer Key)

1. Stop-pot, to
2. Pressure-sure, puree, press, super
3. Limit-tilt
4. Ignore-ring, no, go, in
5. Truth-ruth, run, hut, nut.
6. Minute-ten, nut, in, mint, it, mine, time, net
7. Observe-bee, serve, so, see, bore.
8. Mouth-to, out
9. Example-lamp, me, map, plea, lee, pea, ample, axe, ax, pam
10. Negative-gate, ate, get, give, tea, net, neat, get, gain, ten
11. Time-me, it, Tim

Journal

A Place To Journal Your Thoughts

"My mind escapes as the clouds forms shapes; variations and norms peek my imagination"
– Thomasema Pannell

A Place To Journal Your Thoughts

"Clouds racing fast and fiery; never let your heart become weary"
– Thomasema Pannell

A Place To Journal Your Thoughts

"Blue skies; what a sight to see always bright in my eyes you see"
– Thomasema Pannell

A Place To Journal Your Thoughts

"My heart is warm like the dew drops face the clouds"
- Thomasema Pannell

A Place To Journal Your Thoughts

"Grapes off the vine; I love sunshine; skies bright in the summertime" – Thomasema Pannell

A Place To Journal Your Thoughts

"Look far as you can see; reach far as you can and know that you can" – Thomasema Pannell

A Place To Journal Your Thoughts

"Eagles fly high in the sky; I always ask the question why; shy, bye, cry, or sigh – we are free to fly" – Thomasema Pannell

A Place To Journal Your Thoughts

"Rumble, cloud rushing, humbleness waves the misty sky; no one can say goodbye" – Thomasema Pannell

A Place To Journal Your Thoughts

"When your soul is anchored; clouds raging; warm winds blowing – the sun begins to shine through" – Thomasema Pannell

A Place To Journal Your Thoughts

"Fluffy white cotton balls; out comes the sun"
– Solomon Quick

A Place To Journal Your Thoughts

"Reflections of love; never waiver; endless ripples pushing through sounds of gushing water; strong winds obey" – Thomasema Pannell

Also by Thomasema Pannell

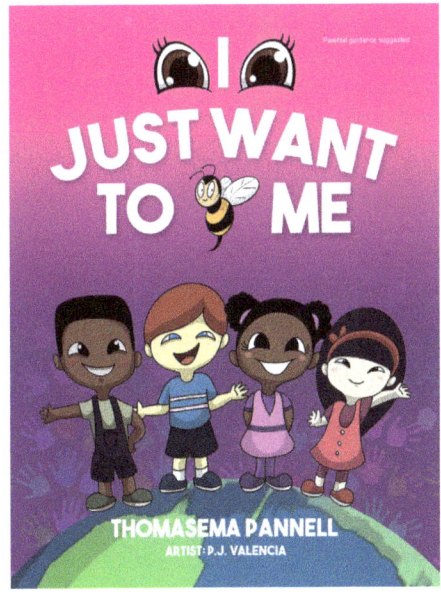

Thomasema Pannell, Biography

Thomasema Pannell, raised in Roosevelt, Long Island, New York. She is retired from the United States Army. She served an honorable twenty-year career while being assigned to numerous Joint Military assignments such as: The White House, White House Communications Agency, The Pentagon (Task Force Russia, POW/MIA, PERSCOM), United States Intelligence & Security Command (INSCOM), and various United States Army installations.

Ms. Pannell is the independent owner of Thomasema Pannell, LLC and a published author of *I Just Want To Be Me, Split Moment,* the novel *Denton Place-Tables Turned and a workbook/journal Denton Place-Letters From The Heart".* She works with certified John C. Maxwell, coach, trainer, and speaker, 2019. She coordinates and co-hosts seminars and workshops like the International Book Signing (July 2018), Book Signing- "Queen In You Conference" (January 2019) in Orlando, Florida, and jointly coordinated and hosted the 2019 "Removing Self-Imposed Barriers" Seminar, at the Embassy Suites, Fayetteville.

Ms. Pannell has earned credit hours from Virginia Union University, an Associate in Science Degree in General Studies from Northern Virginia Community College, a Bachelor of Science in Business Management from National Louis University, a Master of Art in Human Resources Management from Central Michigan University, and she completed more than three years of Doctorate studies in Organizational Leadership from the University of Phoenix.

Ms. Pannell's community activities include the following: membership at Lewis Chapel Missionary Baptist Church (Choir Member, Bible Study, Assist Youth Ministries, and Drive-Thru Prayer Ministry), assisting in the LCMBC-West Site Pastor's Summer Camp and Afterschool Programs, North Carolina Price Hall Affiliate, The Order Of The Eastern Star, Golden Link, Chapter #67, Raeford, NC (Present Associate Matron, Treasurer 2018/2019), Sojourner Truth Tent #770, Fayetteville, NC, and membership of the National Association for the Advancement of Colored People (NAACP).

Ms. Pannell is a Leader of Influence. She has leadership skills, role modeling, persuasive motivating, and community activist.

Visit www.thomasemapannell.com for more information.

Note From The Author

The question, "How Well Do You Know Yourself?" can be the catalyst for change needed in our lives. It can encourage dialogue and initiate steps towards healing.

It is my desired intention to promote positive connections with others, acknowledge those in high-risk positions, and stimulate self-awareness as a means to adding value to our lives.

Remove your self-imposed barriers.

Learn and invite self-awareness to your life!

We Make Good Great

www.butterflytypeface.co